JOHN THOMPSON'S
EASIEST PIANO COURSE

FIRST CHART SONGS

This collection of popular chart songs is intended as supplementary material for those working through **John Thompson's Easiest Piano Course** Parts 2–4. The pieces may also be used for sight reading practice by more advanced students.

Dynamics and phrasing have been deliberately omitted from the earlier pieces, since they are not introduced until Part 3 of the Easiest Piano Course, and initially the student's attention should be focused on playing notes and rhythms accurately. Outline fingering has been included, and in general the hand is assumed to remain in a five-finger position until a new fingering indicates a position shift. The fingering should suit most hands, although logical alternatives are always possible.

The Climb

Words & Music by Jessica Alexander & Jon Mabe

At a quick tempo

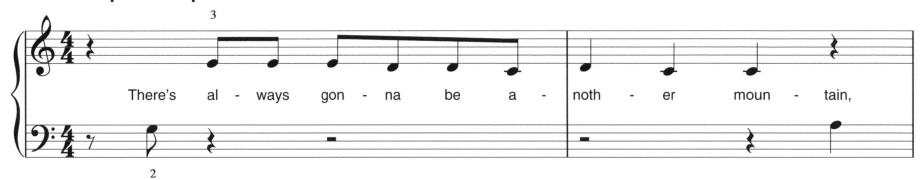

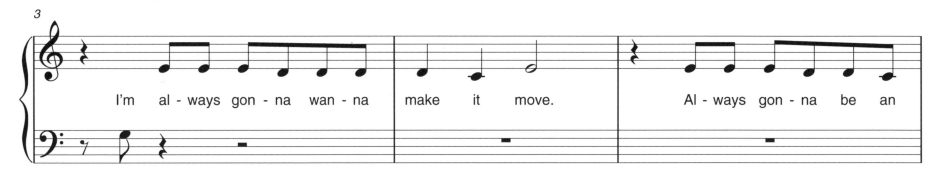

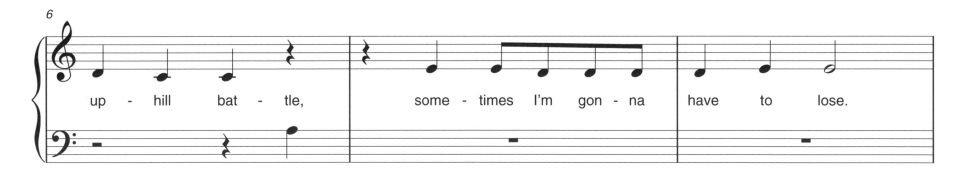

© Copyright 2008 Mabe It Big Music/Music Of Stage Three/Hopeless Rose Music/Vistaville Music/Disney Music Publishing, USA.
Stage Three Music Limited.
All Rights Reserved. International Copyright Secured.

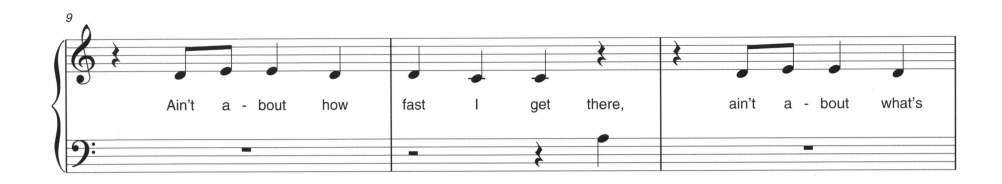

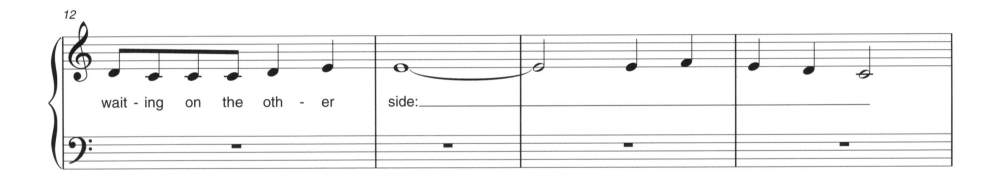

Love Story

Words & Music by Taylor Swift

Steadily

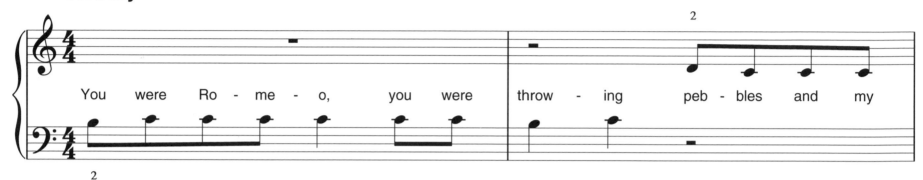

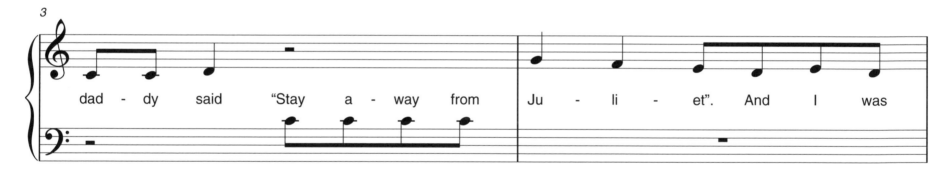

© Copyright 2008 Taylor Swift Music/Sony/ATV Tree Publishing.
Sony/ATV Music Publishing.
All Rights Reserved. International Copyright Secured.

And I said: "Ro - me - o, take___ me some - where we can be a - lone.

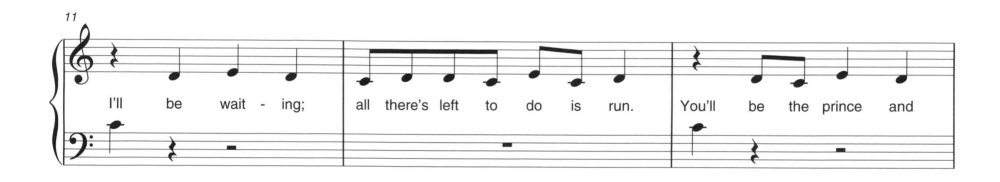

I'll be wait - ing; all there's left to do is run. You'll be the prince and

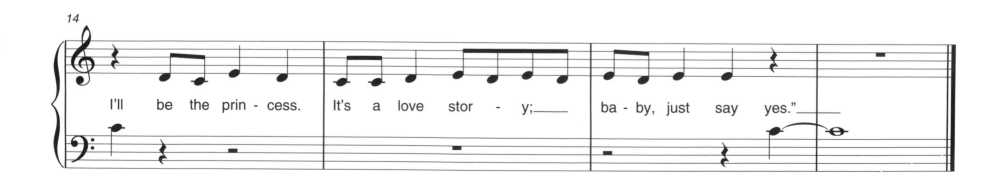

I'll be the prin - cess. It's a love stor - y;___ ba - by, just say yes."___

Viva La Vida

Words & Music by Guy Berryman, Jon Buckland, Will Champion & Chris Martin

Briskly

© Copyright 2008 Universal Music Publishing MGB Limited.
All Rights Reserved. International Copyright Secured.

bells a - ring - ing, Ro - man Cav - al - ry choirs are sing - ing. Be my mir - ror, my

sword, my shield, my mis - sion - ar - ies in a for - eign field._____

For some rea - son, I can't ex - plain, once you'd gone, there was nev - er, nev - er an

hon - est word, and that was when I ruled the world.

My Heart Will Go On (Love Theme from 'Titanic')

Words by Will Jennings & Music by James Horner

Expressively

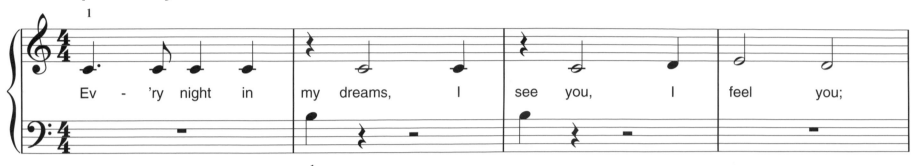

Ev - 'ry night in my dreams, I see you, I feel you;

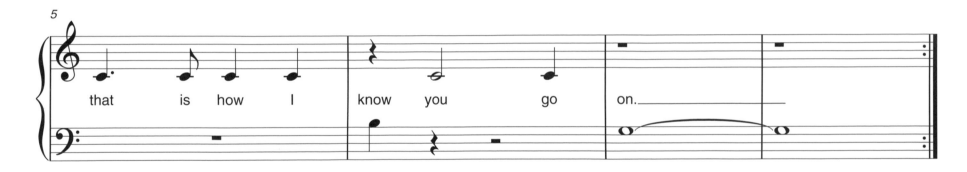

that is how I know you go on.

Near, far, wher - ev - er you are, I be -

© Copyright 1997 Blue Sky Rider Songs/Fox Film Music Corporation/TCF Music Publishing Inc.
Universal Music Publishing Limited/EMI Music Publishing Limited.
All Rights Reserved. International Copyright Secured.

-lieve that the heart does go on._____

Once more, you o - pen the door, and you're

here in my heart, and my heart will go on and on.

9

Eye Of The Tiger

Words & Music by Jim Peterik & Frank Sullivan III

Menacingly

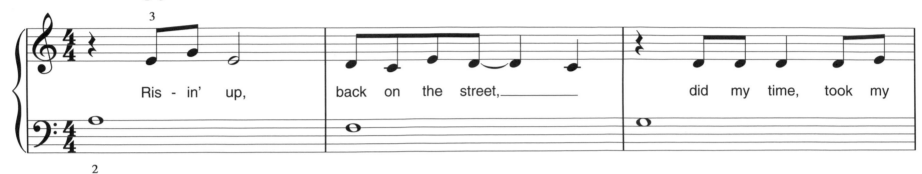

© Copyright 1982 Three Wise Boys Music LLC/W.B. Music Corporation/Easy Action Music.
Warner/Chappell Music Limited/Famous Music Publishing Limited.
All Rights Reserved. International Copyright Secured.

thrill of the fight,____ ri - sing up to the chal - lenge of our ri - val. And the

last known sur - vi - vor stalks his prey in the night,____ and he's watch - ing us all with the

eye of the ti - ger, the eye of the ti - ger.____

(Sittin' On) The Dock Of The Bay

Words & Music by Otis Redding & Steve Cropper

Relaxedly

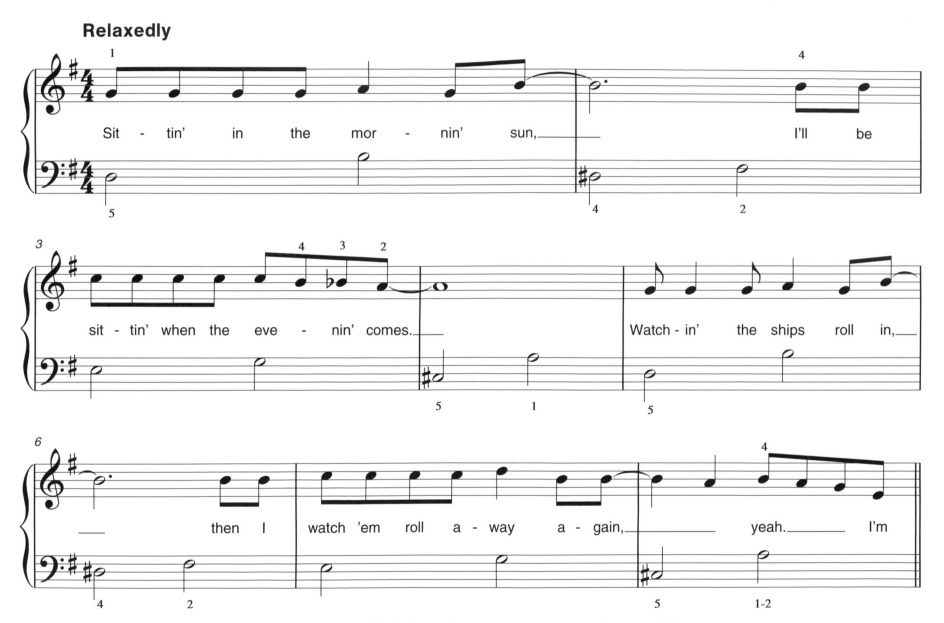

© Copyright 1967 East Memphis Music Corporation/Irving Music Corporation/Cotillion Music Incorporated, USA.
Rondor Music International (administered in Germany by Rondor Musikverlag GmbH)/Warner/Chappell Music Limited.
All Rights Reserved. International Copyright Secured.

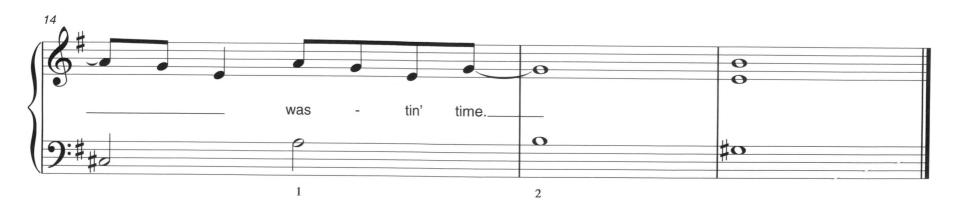

Eternal Flame

Words & Music by Susanna Hoffs, Tom Kelly & Billy Steinberg

With feeling

© Copyright 1988 & 1989 Sony/ATV Tunes LLC/Bangophile Music.
Sony/ATV Music Publishing/Universal Music Publishing Limited.
All Rights Reserved. International Copyright Secured.

Just Dance

Words & Music by Aliaune Thiam, Stefani Germanotta & Nadir Khayat

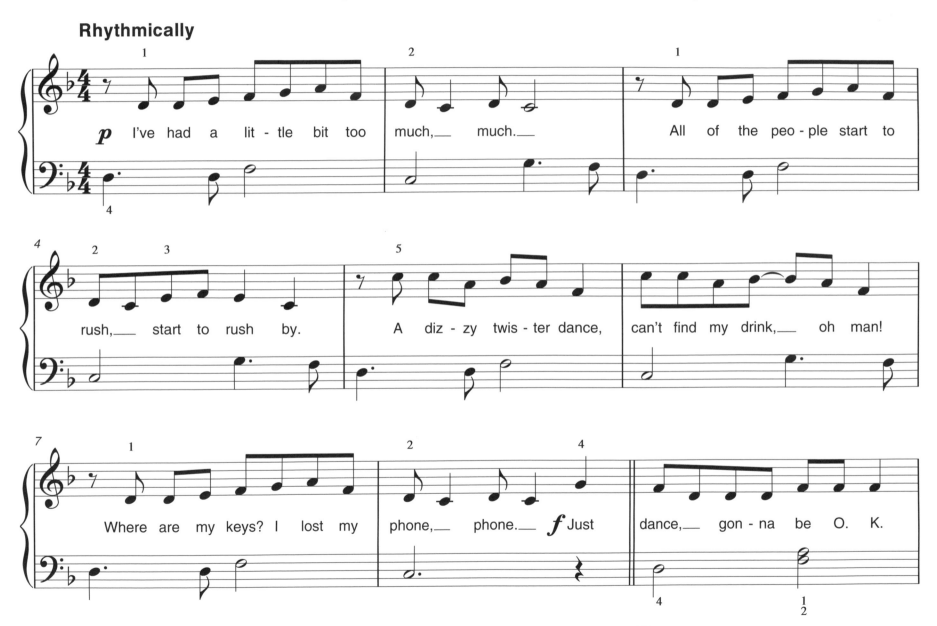

© Copyright 2008 Byefall Productions Incorporated/Sony ATV Songs LLC/Sony/ATV Harmony, USA.
Sony/ATV Music Publishing.
All Rights Reserved. International Copyright Secured.

16

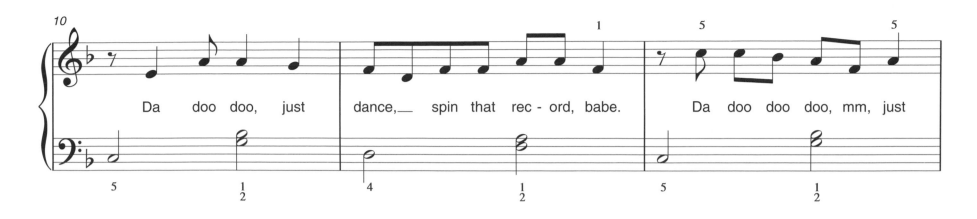

If I Were A Boy

Words & Music by Toby Gad & Brittany Carlson

© Copyright 2008 BMG Ruby Songs (ASCAP),Liedela Music (ASCAP),Gad Songs LLC (ASCAP), Songs Of Universal, Inc. (BMI) and BC Jean (BMI).
Worldwide Rights for BMG Ruby Songs, Liedela Music and Gad Songs LLC Administered by BMG Rights Management (US) LLC.
All Rights for BC Jean Controlled and Administered by Songs of Universal, Inc. All Rights Reserved. International Copyright Secured.

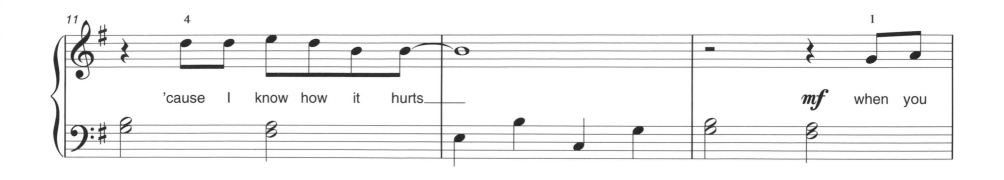

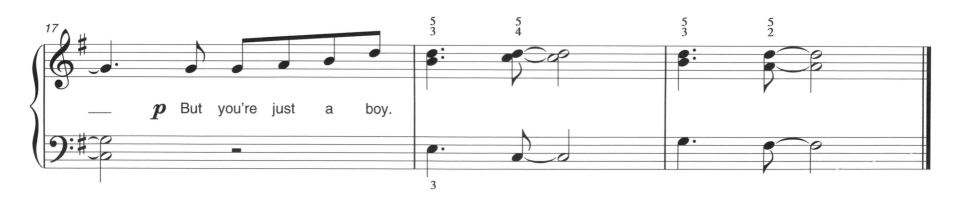

Broken Strings

Words & Music by James Morrison, Fraser T. Smith & Nina Woodford

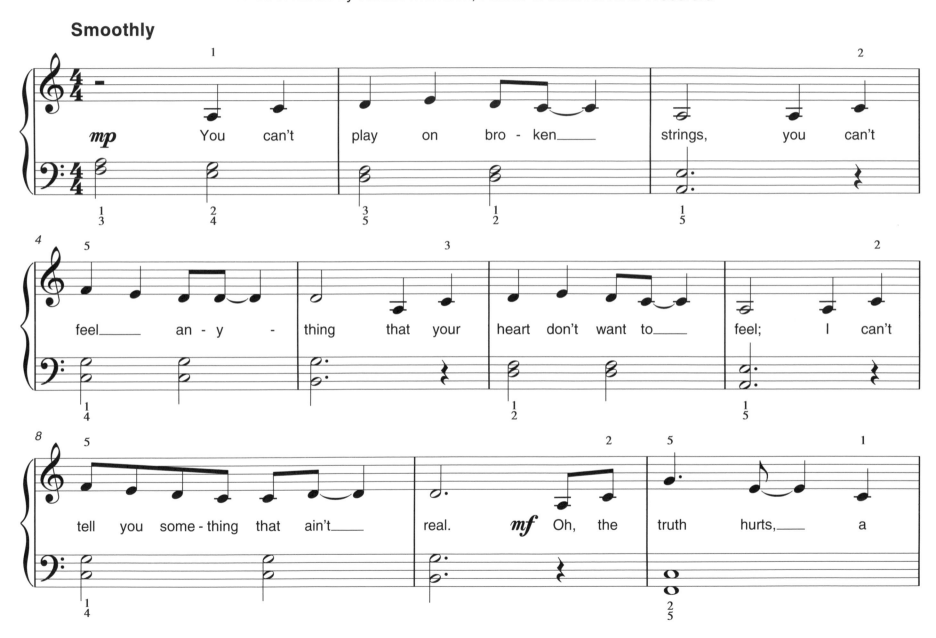

© Copyright 2008 Chrysalis Music Limited/Sony/ATV Music Publishing.
All Rights Reserved. International Copyright Secured.

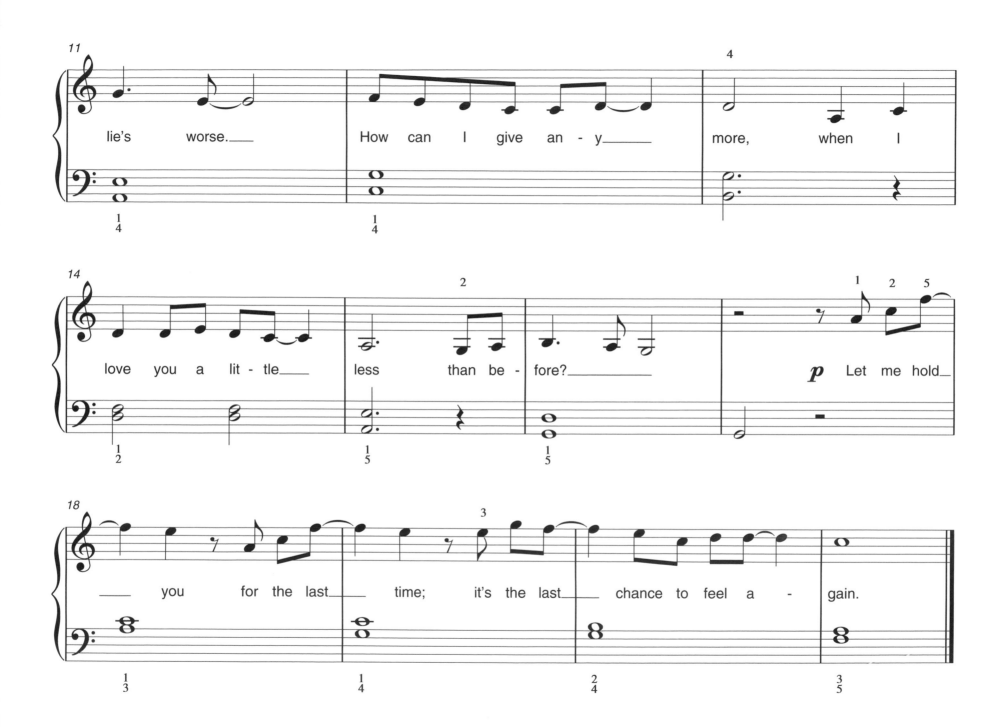

Rolling In The Deep

Words & Music by Paul Epworth & Adele Adkins

With a driving beat

© Copyright 2010, 2011 Universal Music Publishing Ltd/EMI Music Publishing Ltd.
All Rights Reserved. International Copyright Secured.

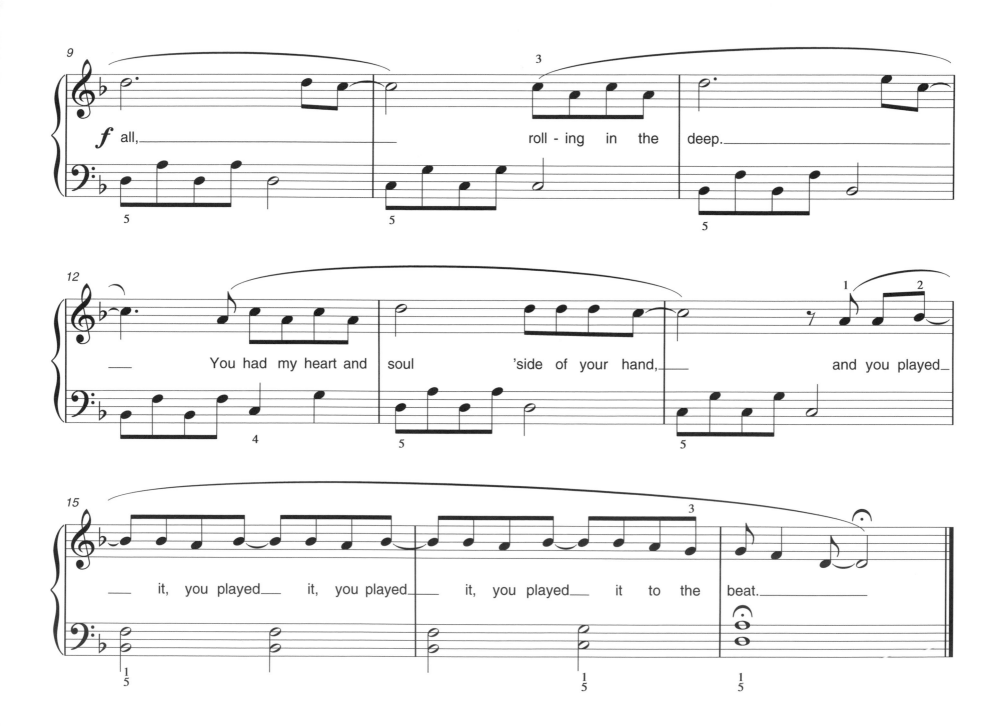

Hallelujah

Words & Music by Leonard Cohen

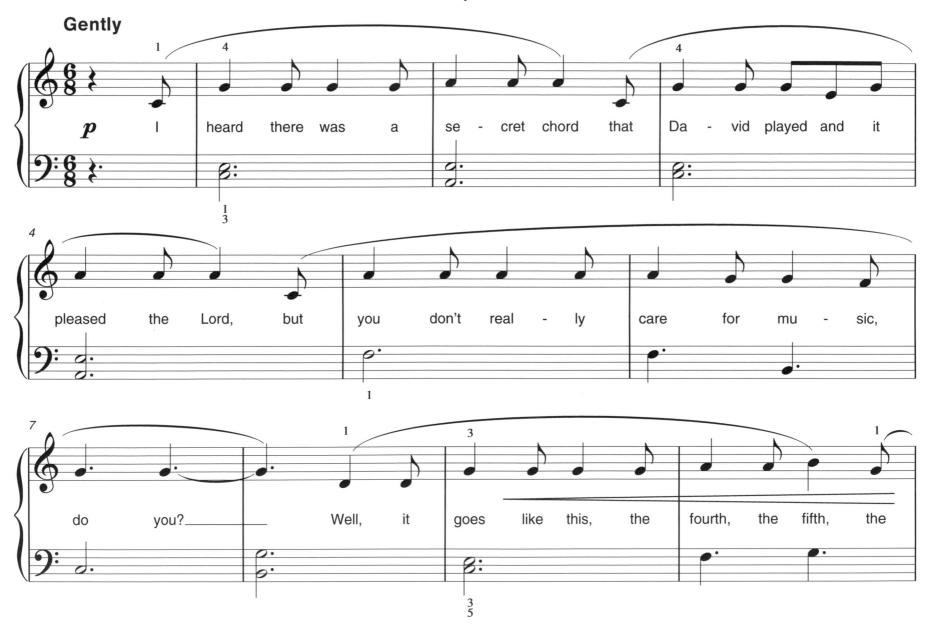

© Copyright 1984 Sony/ATV Music Publishing.
All Rights Reserved. International Copyright Secured.

You're Beautiful

Words & Music by Sacha Skarbek, James Blunt & Amanda Ghost

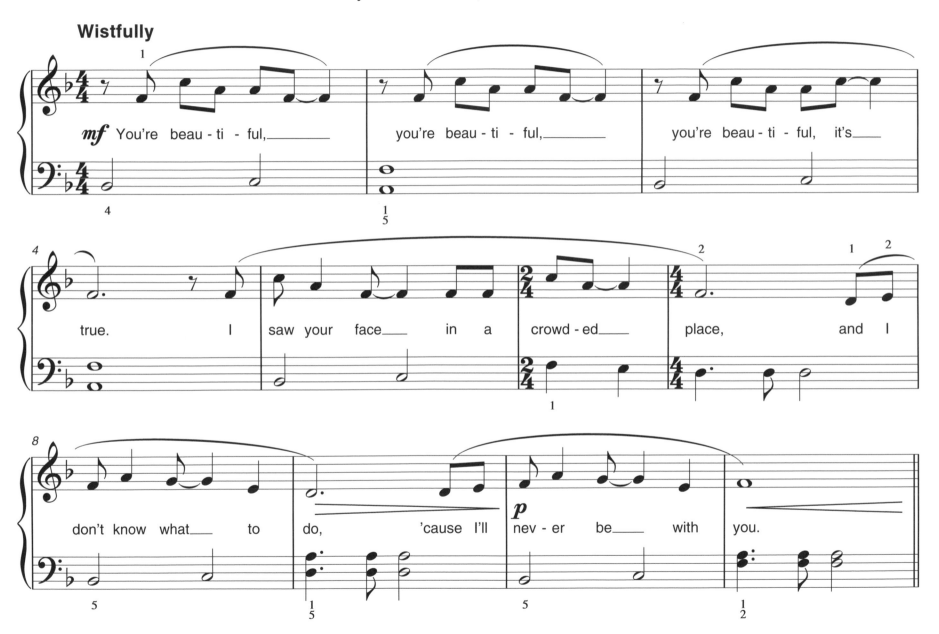

© Copyright 2004 EMI Music Publishing Limited/Bucks Music Group Limited.
All Rights Reserved. International Copyright Secured.

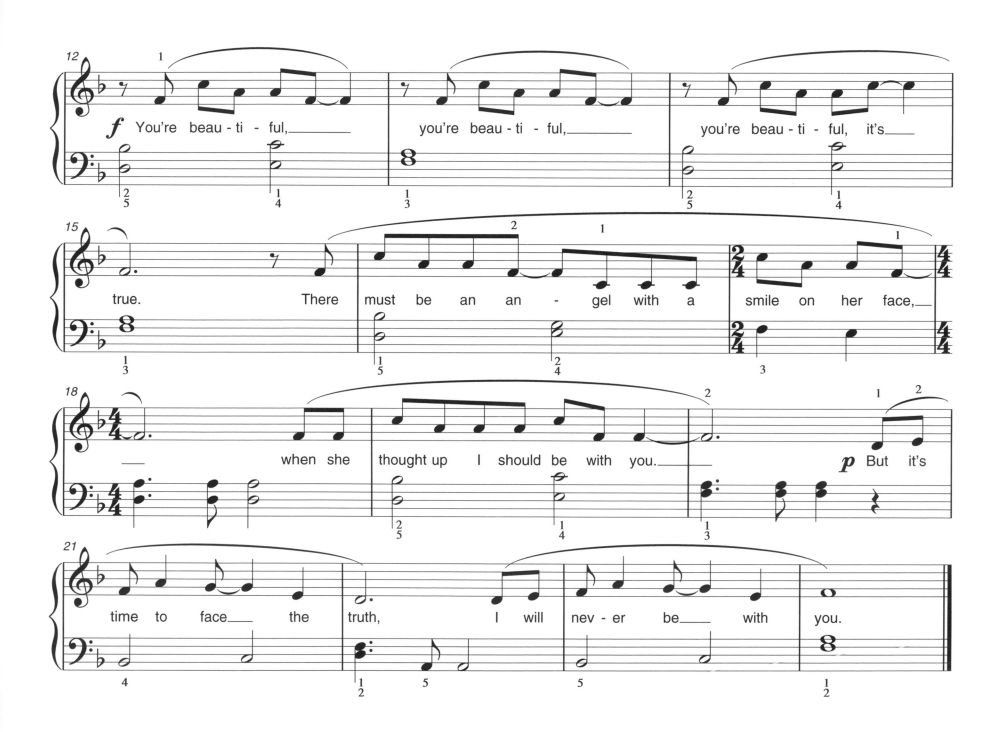

Just The Way You Are

Words & Music by Ari Levine, Bruno Mars, Philip Lawrence, Khari Cain & Khalil Walton

© Copyright 2010 Universal Music Corporation, USA/Art For Art's Sake Music/Toy Plane Music/Upper Dec,
USA/Roc Nation Music, USA/Music Famamanem, USA/Mars Force Music, USA/Northside Independent Music Publishing, USA/Music Of Windswept.
Bug Music Limited/Warner/Chappell North America Limited/Universal/MCA Music Limited/Bug Music (Windswept Account).
All Rights Reserved. International Copyright Secured.

I Will Always Love You

Words & Music by Dolly Parton

Slowly and tenderly

If____ I should____ stay, I would on - ly be in your way.____ So, I'll____ go, but I know I'll think of you ev - 'ry step of the way.____ And I____

© Copyright 1973 Velvet Apple Music, USA.
Carlin Music Corporation for the world (excluding Germany, Austria, Switzerland, Scandinavia, Eastern Europe, Australia, New Zealand, Japan, South Africa, Canada and the United States of America).
All Rights Reserved. International Copyright Secured.

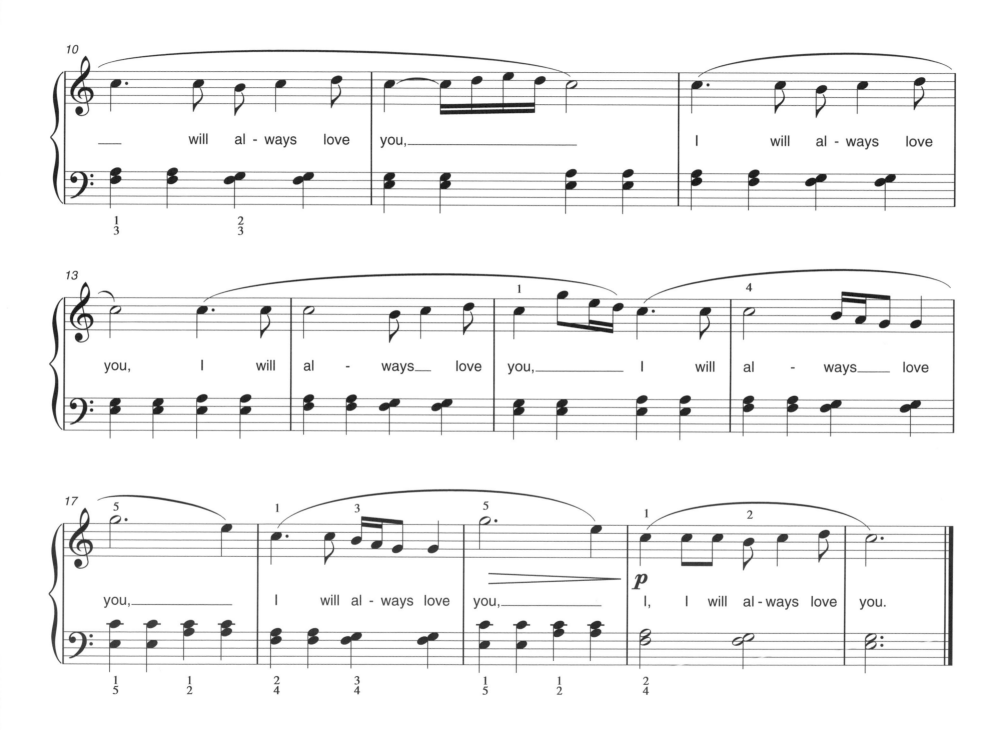

© Copyright 2013 The Willis Music Company
Florence, Kentucky, USA. All Rights Reserved.

Exclusive Distributors:
Hal Leonard
7777 West Bluemound Road,
Milwaukee, WI 53213
Email: info@halleonard.com
Hal Leonard Europe Limited
42 Wigmore Street,
Marylebone, London WIU 2 RY
Email: info@halleonardeurope.com
Hal Leonard Australia Pty. Ltd.
4 Lentara Court, Cheltenham,
Victoria 9132, Australia
Email: info@halleonard.com.au

Order No. WMR101299R
ISBN: 978-1-78305-316-2

For all works contained herein:
Unauthorized copying, arranging, adapting, recording, Internet
posting, public performance, or other distribution of the music in this
publication is an infringement of copyright. Infringers are liable under
the law.

Arranged by Christopher Hussey.
Arrangements and engravings supplied by Camden Music Services.
Edited by Sam Lung.

Printed in the EU.